My Mom is a Nurse Anesthetist

by Jeffrey D Heese

My Mom is a Nurse Anesthetist

ISBN: 9798701821529

Dedicated to Traci.
My favorite nurse anesthetist.

Hi! I'm Jamie.
I want to tell you
about a really smart
and pretty person.
My Mom!

A long time ago, Mom decided that she wanted to help people when they weren't feeling well. She decided to go to nursing school. There, she learned how to help people by giving medicines, changing bandages, helping people breathe better, and teaching people how to live healthier.

SCHOOL OF NURSING

My Mom worked hard in school. She would go to the hospital during the day to work with patients and doctors, and in the evening, she would go to the library and read for her classes. It was a lot of work.

After she finished school, Mom took one last test to become a registered nurse. The test makes sure people working as nurses are able to take good care of people.

Then, Mom worked for a
hospital where she took
care of people. Mom was
one of the best nurses,
and because of that she
would work with people
who needed a lot of help.

Even though Mom liked caring for the patients at her hospital, she knew there were ways she could help more people. After talking to many people, she thought becoming a nurse anesthetist would be the best way she could help.

Nurse anesthetists take care of people during surgery. When a doctor needs to operate on a person, the nurse anesthetist makes sure the patient does not hurt. They also help the person not to feel afraid.

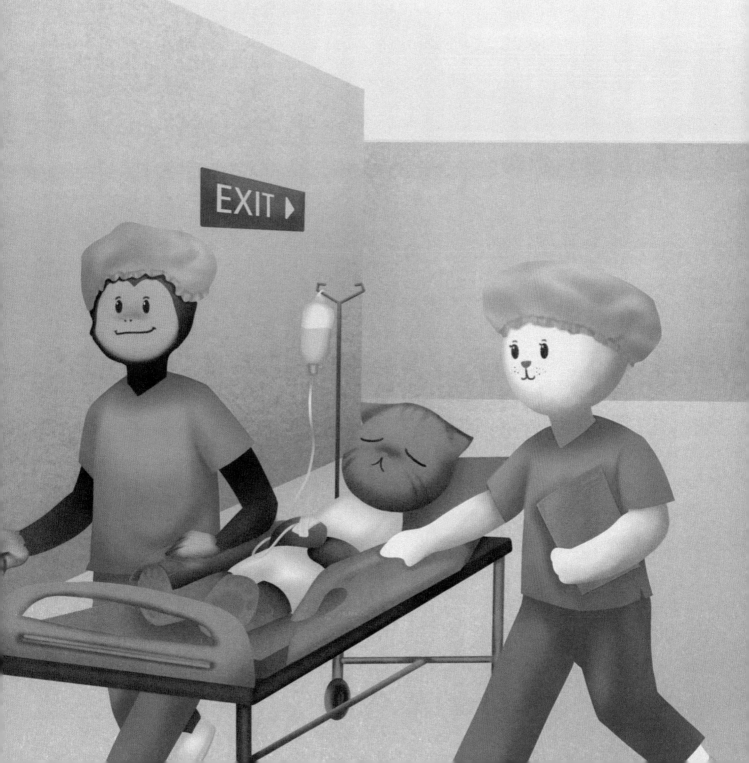

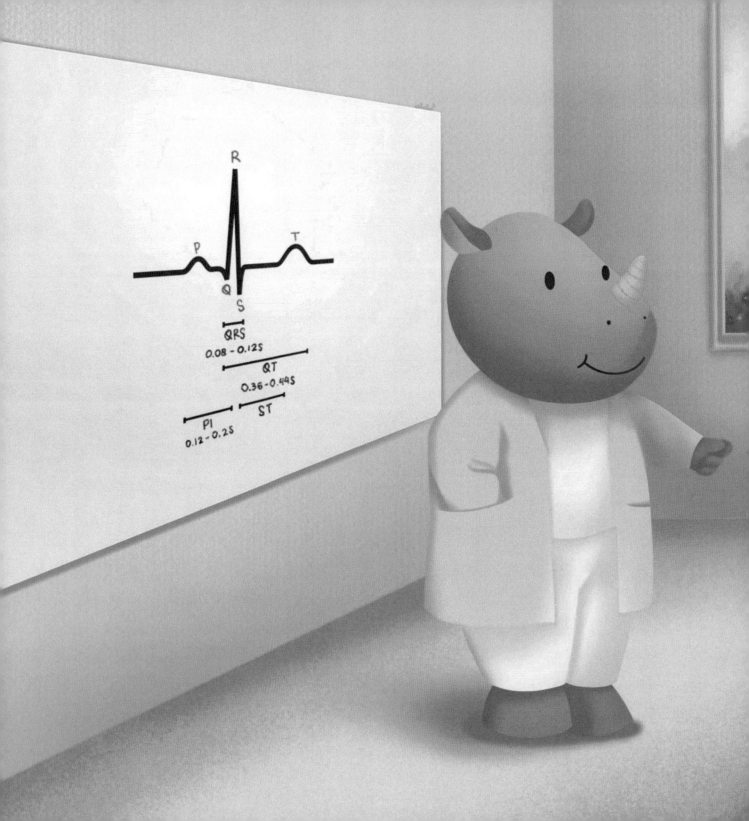

Mom went to school again to learn how to be a nurse anesthetist. This school was very hard. But my Mom did her best, because she knew what she was learning would help her take good care of people.

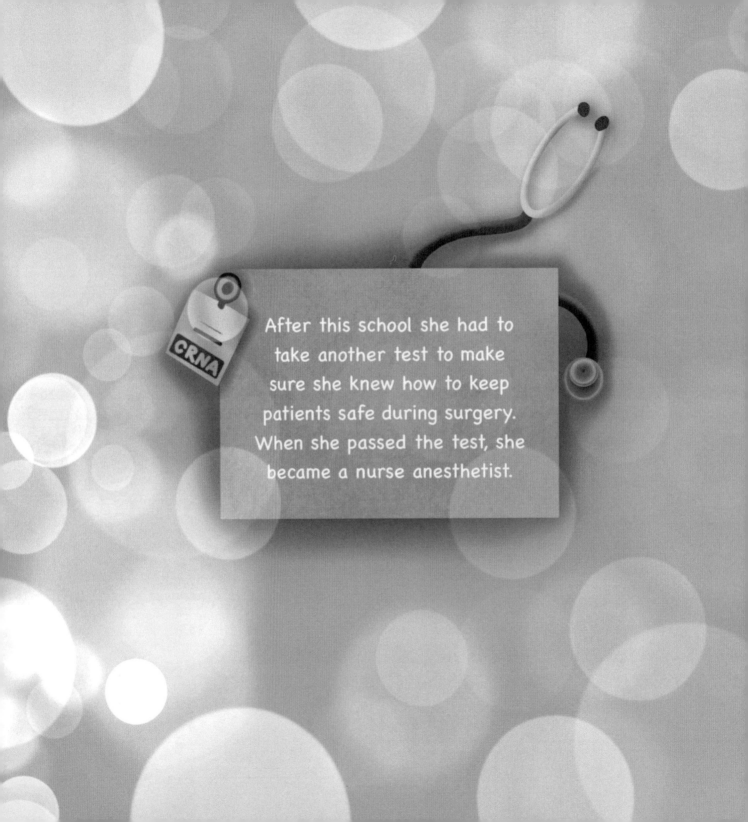

After this school she had to take another test to make sure she knew how to keep patients safe during surgery. When she passed the test, she became a nurse anesthetist.

Now my mom helps people every day. She makes sure they don't hurt and that they feel safe. I am very proud of her. I hope that someday, I can have a job that helps people too.

There are lots of jobs where you work with people to help them live healthier lives. These jobs are very important. From the list below do you see any jobs that are done by people you know? Do you see any jobs that you might want to do someday yourself?

Nurse
Doctor
Pharmacist
Respiratory Therapist
Surgical Technologist
Nurse Midwife
Nutritionist

If you don't know what these jobs are you can ask a parent or older friend to help you. There are also videos that explain these jobs.

Hi there! I'm Lucy, and this is my brother Cosmo. We're Jamie's neighbors. If you liked learning about what nurse anesthetists do, we're sure you would LOVE to hear about our mom too.

Our Mom is a Pharmacist!

Look for our new book to learn about another great healthcare profession.

Hope to see
you soon!

Made in the USA
Las Vegas, NV
05 February 2024

85341859R00017